Alexei Maxim Russell's

Field Guide to Assholes

ALEXEI MAXIM RUSSELL

Published by Why Not-World dot com

TABLE OF CONTENTS

INTRODUCTION

 Have you ever considered taking up the sport of asshole-watching? Much like bird-watching or a trip to the safari park, asshole-watching can be both fun and educational. And, what is more, a thorough knowledge of assholes--their habits, how to identify them and how to best repel their attacks--is an essential skill to learn, for anyone who hopes to make their way through life, asshole-free.

This authoritative field guide will ensure that your asshole-watching experience is as safe and informative as possible, through handy tips and the thorough asshole-related knowledge that can only come from extensive life experience. So, whether you are starting in a new job, in a cut-throat industry, or are planning to re-enter the dating scene, or just want to help an asshole friend to reach a better level of self-awareness, you are going to need a guide. With this handy book, the aspiring asshole-watcher can learn to spot all the different varieties of assholery, just like a pro!

As a writer, and an enthusiastic observer of human behavior, my research has taken me into a variety of strange and foreign destinations. Far and wide, I've researched assholery, in the hopes of better educating the public. The result is this book, which, I hope, will help all good and decent human beings to avoid the perilous pitfalls of assholery and all the harm, both physical and psychological, which can result from an incomplete understanding of assholes. In addition, I hope to assist those people who may be tempted to a life of asshole behavior, to reconsider their path, through the knowledge they gain, here, about just how harmful an asshole can be, both to himself and the people around him. If you find yourself at this dark and antisocial crossroads, I suggest that you also study another one of my titles, "Instruction Manual for the 21st Century Samurai." This book serves as an ideal companion-piece, for this book, and should help to lead you in the direction of how to behave with the dignity, decency, strength of character, and the gentlemanly behavior that usually accompanies fully-grown mannishness--and so help you to avoid the sorrows and pitfalls of the asshole life. It is my sincere desire that my research and hard work will help create a world where we may all learn to walk this Earth, safe, enlightened and free from the perils of cruelty, ignorance, and all the other dark and sinister forces, which make assholes possible.

With Love and Respect,

Alexei Maxim Russell

"We don't devote enough scientific research
to finding a cure for jerks."

Bill Waterson

THE ARROGANT PRICK

If you hear a loud, obnoxious call, echoing over the meadows, you may have come within hearing range of an Arrogant Prick. This variety of asshole is all too common,  unfortunately, but is most likely to be found in the city. Their natural habitats include boardrooms, the corridors of power and any place where fame, admiration and adoring crowds are to be found. Since these things are not common in the country, it is recommended you look for them in a big city. They are usually to be found at the top of the food chain, and the observant asshole-watcher can often witness them, devouring and destroying lesser mammals, either for fun or sustenance.

Likely Occupations: Upper Management, Football Player, Famous Musician.

How to Identify: An Arrogant Prick can mainly be identified by the noise he makes. The loudest of all assholes, it's impossible to ignore their booming call, even from twenty yards away, or more. They can often be found, talking loudly in high-end restaurants or making obnoxious comments to the serving staff, at your local bar. When in the proximity of a potential mate, the Arrogant Prick will exhibit an even more alarming and fear-inducing mating call. This call has been described as a cross between a wolverine caught in a steel trap and category five hurricane. Scientists believe this call has been specially evolved, by the Arrogant Prick, to stun potential mates into submission, before being dragged away and imprisoned in their ostentatious penthouse condos. You can also identify Arrogant Pricks by their tastelessly gaudy appearance. They are prone to wear expensive suits, opulent rings on their fingers and often sport toupees. They are also prone to drive expensive cars and are likely to exude the musky scent of far too much cologne. Lastly, the Arrogant Prick can be identified by the feral, beastly look he'll give you, whenever you make eye contact. They are predatory animals, and look upon everyone and everything as potential prey. It is recommended, therefore, that you do not make eye contact with an Arrogant Prick.

Social Habits: Keen observers of the Arrogant Prick have determined their primary motivation to be a need for adoration. They crave respect, admiration and popularity and if this means bullying or whipping those around them, in order to make themselves look superior, then they will not hesitate to do so. They like nothing better than to boast, brag and make those around them feel as inferior as possible. In response to this barrage of aggressive conceit, most people will either walk away, feeling hurt, or submit to the Arrogant Prick's vie for dominance, and so become one of his followers. They will often have droves of followers, as a result. Arrogant Pricks can often be found in corporate environments, surrounded by "yes men" or at the head of a music group, surrounded by adoring fans. This is the ideal environment, for the Arrogant Prick and they will become very territorial, after establishing themselves as the head of a pack. It is recommended that you not approach an Arrogant

Prick, in any situation, but especially when they are established as the head of a pack of followers, as they could become very aggressive. The asshole-watcher is advised to keep a safe distance and use binoculars or field glasses, to observe them from afar.

How to Repel an Attack: If you have been unfortunate enough to get too close to an Arrogant Prick, or to have inadvertently challenged him through accidental eye contact, then you will surely find yourself facing the brunt of his aggressive conceit. This is a very frightening situation to be in, because an enraged Arrogant Prick is extremely unpredictable. If you find yourself in this situation, don't panic. By understanding the psychology of this asshole, you can escape his wrath without too much trouble. Keep in mind that when it comes to the Arrogant Prick, their bark is much worse than their bite. They are actually more scared of you, then you are of them. Because they are motivated by fame, respect and popularity, this means they are very fearful of being unpopular or publicly shamed. They are terrified, at every moment, that someone might expose them for the imposter they are. Since their popularity and authority are based on bullying and aggression, rather than merit, they are keenly aware of the fact that they don't really deserve the adoration of their followers. This is why they live in constant fear of a challenge, and will be very protective of their position. In order to free yourself from an Arrogant Prick attack, therefore, you need to threaten him with public shaming or some other form of disgrace, which would mean a decrease in popularity. If you are a member of a prestigious social group or a journalist with media contacts, then you can use this affiliation to cow the asshole into submission. As loudly as they bark, they will quickly submit, when in fear of exposure or public shaming. If you are not a member of any "in crowd", then you can at least bluff and imply that you are. As impressive as they may seem, Arrogant Pricks are rarely intelligent. Above all, it is important to never submit to the Arrogant Prick's vie for dominance. You must either threaten them with some form of social disgrace or feign calm and meet their onslaught bravely, until you can get out of their proximity. The worst thing you can do is show fear. Arrogant Pricks can smell fear, and it makes them salivate.

THE SHADY SCUMBAG

Under the cover of darkness, or hidden away under a rock, lurks the Shady Scumbag. This variety of asshole is a shy, yet lethal, creature who only emerges from the safety of his hole, when there is something to be stolen, defiled or violated. However, they will only poke their head out of their lair if they are one hundred percent certain that no one is watching. Cowardly by nature, their natural habitats include shady back lanes or quiet, secluded places, where they can lie in wait for the unwary traveller, or the naïve, trusting fool.

Likely Occupations: Black Market Vendor, Lower Management, Petty Thief.

How to Identify: Of all the assholes, the Shady Scumbag is one of the most difficult to spot. This is because they are usually cleverly camouflaged, to blend in with the scenery. Timid and easily frightened, they will invariably hide under a veneer of respectability. It is not until you are alone and unprotected, that he will show himself for what he is-- a shameless opportunist, with no respect for the rights of other people. He will often be spotted, for a fleeting moment, by the vigilant asshole-watcher, cutting you off in traffic or pushing in line at the bank, ahead of an old lady who he knows is too frail to fight back. Because of his timidity and his tendency to camouflage himself, the Shady Scumbag can only really be identified by how he treats those who are weaker than himself. If you put the Shady Scumbag next to a kid with a candy cane, and leave him alone, for a minute, you'll probably find both the asshole and the candy has vanished, by the time you get back. Don't trust him with your grandmother's purse or to drive home your drunk sister, either, because the Shady Scumbag lives to get away with crimes, no matter how lowdown and petty. Having no compassion or empathy, it is only the law which keeps him in line and the one thing which stops him from becoming a more serious criminal is his inherent cowardice.

<u>Social Habits:</u> The primary motivation of the Shady Scumbag is to get away with a crime, and so benefit himself. Unlike the Sadistic Bastard or the Diabolical Sicko, they are not necessarily out to hurt anybody. They just don't give a damn about anybody, which is why they won't hesitate to steal your wallet, if you're foolish enough to leave it, unattended, in their presence. They probably know that you'll be upset about it, but they don't care. And besides, the benefit to them outweighs anything that may happen to you, in their opinion. Because they are motivated by greed and acquisition, they will often be found in positions of trust, where they can start grabbing, the moment everyone's back is turned. The bank manager who embezzles the bank's funds, or the lecherous university professor, who exploits his naïve students, to satisfy his wicked wants are two excellent examples of Shady Scumbags, in their ideal social habitat. As has been stated, it is hard to identify this variety of asshole, because they are so good at hiding in plain sight. They can assume any shape and simulate any form, in order to inveigle their way into a position of trust, and so, they are capable of taking any form, socially, and exhibiting any variety of social habits. The only clues

you may get is that Shady Scumbags do not like to make waves. Unlike the Arrogant Prick, they are likely to be quiet and unassuming--average, even. This personality predisposes them towards a job as a lower or middle manager. Someone who doesn't need to stand out, but also has enough power to take full advantage, behind closed doors. What's more, they are easily identified by their complete lack of compassion. If you get them into a situation where a normal, healthy human being would feel pity, sympathy or remorse, they will exhibit none of the above.

How to Repel and Attack: If you are under attack by a Shady Scumbag, then you are probably either under anesthetic or shackled to the wall. In which case, you have good reason to be afraid. Because, although they only attack when their victim is unable to fight back, they will be completely without mercy, when once they have you in their trap. The best defence against the Shady Scumbag is to be vigilant at all times and ensure, ahead of time, that you are well able to defend yourself. This variety of asshole would never even step into the same room with a karate black-belt, if he could help it, let alone try to rob him, so a knowledge of self-defence is pretty much guaranteed to repel the Shady Scumbag, in any and all circumstances. If, however, you have been foolish enough to tread into his dark alley, after having one too many Martinis, and have left your back open to his wicked little claws, then you really have no option but to try to defend yourself. Screaming loudly or roaring like a lion might work wonders. Do not ask for mercy, because he has none to offer you. Your only chance lies in intimidation. After all, there is one trait that you can trust in, completely, when it comes to the Shady Scumbag. You can trust in their deep and enduring cowardice. For the spineless Scumbag, any form of opposition will invariably be met with fear.

THE SLICK SOCIOPATH

When hiking through thick grasses, the dedicated asshole-watcher should take great care to avoid the slithering and quick-tongued Slick Sociopath. This variety of asshole can often pounce upon you, unexpected, and capture you in its maw, before you even know what happened. For this reason, it is wise to step carefully, as the Slick Sociopath is only safe to view from a distance. They can usually be found in marketplaces, sales showrooms or any place where naïve people congregate. The cautious asshole-watcher can observe the skill in which this cunning predator lulls his victim into a false sense of security, before sinking his fangs in, for the kill. It is important to stay out of earshot, however, as the haunting call of the Slick Sociopath has been known to charm even the strongest minds, leaving their victim weak-willed and senseless, and open to the Sociopath's wicked, blood-sucking wiles.

<u>Likely Occupations:</u> Salesperson, Entrepreneur, Cult Leader.

<u>How to Identify:</u> The Slick Sociopath can be identified by his immaculate hygiene, his flashy suit, his sonorous song and his fake smile. The charm of this variety of asshole is legendary. They can cast a hypnotic spell over their victim, by using a mixture of pleasing appearance, charming words and an above average level of social skill. They can most often be found in retail environments, or any place where a sale can be made. The observant asshole-watcher can see scores of Slick Sociopaths at major sales events or in used car lots. But cold hard cash isn't the only prize, which the Slick Sociopath chases after. They can often be found serving as the charismatic leader of an organization, or at a singles bar, using their natural charms to secure a mate. Unlike the Arrogant Prick, however, the Slick Sociopath will use his immaculate charm to lure his victim into his lair. And, unlike the Arrogant Prick, whose victim may resent having been

bullied into submission, the Slick Sociopath will brainwash his mate with consummate skill, utilizing well-practiced social manipulation tactics, to trick them into believing that they brought it on themselves, somehow, or that he did them a favor, in fact, by abusing them. When observing the Slick Sociopath, it is important to note that not all people who exhibit these traits are Slick Sociopaths. Some of them are regular people and not actually assholes. For example, the charismatic head of a start-up company may, in fact, just be a skilled salesman with above average social skill and not an asshole at all. The perceptive asshole-watcher is advised to pay close attention to how these powers of persuasion are being used. If they are being used for selfish ends, to get as much as possible out of other people, then you are, indeed, looking at an asshole. If great social skills and immaculate charm are being used for honest ends, then you may have mistakenly caught sight of a regular human being. It is important to avoid this common mistake, when observing this type of asshole.

Social Habits: The Slick Sociopath is motivated entirely by his desire to manipulate you, and so get what he wants. He wants to get as much as he possibly can, out of the people who surround him. Unlike regular human beings, who can appreciate a person, simply for their company or their friendship, this variety of asshole is concerned with only one thing: how much he can squeeze out of you. If you have money, he'll use his charm to convince you to give it to him; if he desires you, romantically, he'll bombard you with every persuasive line in his arsenal, until he gets you; if you have nothing to give but your dedicated devotion, he'll take that too! There's really nothing, no matter how small, that he won't try to take from you, if he can. So, in a social sense, the Slick Sociopath is the one you'll find at the social function, collecting followers and hustling the room. He is not an introvert, by any means, so the most natural social habitat for the Slick Sociopath is a busy social environment, like a cocktail party or a casino. He is a highly sociable creature, whose sole mission is to mine the fields of social fortune, to acquire whatever he can. He may seem like a "good guy" who is loads of fun, but the fact is, once he's gotten what he wants out of you, he'll drop you like a bad habit. He has no interest in you, as a person, but only in what you have to offer him. So, any interaction with the Slick Sociopath is certain to end badly. He always sucks his victims dry, eventually, before invariably abandoning them. This is why it is advised that you never observe the Slick Sociopath at close quarters, where you can hear his beguiling sales pitch. Keep your distance and observe him from afar.

How to Repel Attack: If you have been careless enough to step into the natural habitat of the Slick Sociopath and find yourself ensnared in the webs of their charming banter, then it is suggested that you cover your ears and run for the nearest exit. Although not dangerous, in a physical sense, their ability to bewitch your senses and rob you of your free will is a very real danger, which could easily lead you open to their blood-sucking fangs. The only sure fire way to resist a Slick Sociopath attack is to never get close enough for them to talk to you. If the hapless asshole-watcher has been caught unawares, however, and has already succumbed to the Slick Sociopath's charms, then it will no longer be possible to run. The asshole will have robbed you of the ability to think for yourself. At this point, the only hope you have is to threaten them with their greatest fear. Although they are accustomed to talking their way out of trouble, they live in mortal fear of police, media or any other group of people who are not easily fooled. There is no worse nightmare, for the Slick Sociopath, than for their many crimes to be outlined and exposed, to the general public. This would make the entire world wise to their tricks and make all hopes of future manipulation impossible. Although this kind of grand exposure is very unlikely to happen, it is still the Slick Sociopath's worst nightmare. So, it can be used to scare them away, if you ever find yourself caught in their grip. If you have any friends or family in law enforcement, media or the legal profession, be sure to let the asshole know about it. Given their fears, this alone may be enough to repel their attack and scare them far enough away for you to make your escape.

THE CONTROLLING JERK

In the hills and the valleys, many timid creatures roam. They graze the grasses and water at the streams, living a life of peace and harmony. And for every peaceful doe, which roams the tranquil meadows, there is a Controlling Jerk, on the prowl, looking for someone to dominate. If you observe closely, you can spot this ubiquitous asshole, creeping the bars and pick up spots, on the scent of their next victim. Unlike other varieties, this type of asshole preys almost exclusively on females. They revel in the animalistic delight of finding a weak-willed female, and making a veritable slave out of her. Unlike the Arrogant Prick, however, who is obviously dominant, by nature, the Controlling Jerk may appear to be outgoing, average or even shy. They will usually go to great pains to lull their victim into a false sense of security, by doing the right things and saying what is needed, to gain their trust. But, once they feel they have the upper hand, they will change. Once they have done so, their true nature will be revealed, and it will be obvious to even the novice asshole-watcher, that they are a Controlling Jerk. Once in a position of dominance, this asshole can be very dangerous. In fact, when mixed with a little bit of The Diabolical Sicko or the Sadistic Bastard, this can be one of the most dangerous variety of assholes, in all of nature's kingdom.

Likely Occupations: Prison Guard, Independent Contractor, anything involving guns.

How to Identify: This fearsome predator can be most easily identified by the company it keeps. The shrewd asshole-watcher will notice the proximity of a timid, submissive female, somewhere in the Controlling Jerk's immediate vicinity. They never let their victims roam far, and will never let them out of their sight. So, she is almost certain to be nearby. If not in his immediate vicinity, then check his lair. This type of asshole has a strong preference for their mates to be housewives and homemakers, rather than having a career. If the asshole in question has a career-woman as a wife, then you may want to consider that you've made a mistake. This could simply be an obsessive compulsive human being, with a few hang ups, and not an honest-to-goodness Controlling Jerk. The genuine asshole would never let their mate have a career, or do anything that necessitates their leaving the house, unescorted. Their natural habitats include gun shows, military surplus stores and any other place where you might find a heavy duty pick-up truck or a hummer. They tend to like military or para-military events or entertainment, and will possibly even sport some type of military accessory, even if they have never served in such an organization. Being obsessed with control and dominance, they are apt to be preppers, hording food and ammunition in preparation for the day when "the man" decides to come and wrest control of their household away from them. Unlike most other varieties of asshole, the Controlling Jerk is likely to be armed, and may possess an arsenal of different weapons. It is advised, therefore, that the prudent asshole-watcher steer clear of the asshole's lair. This type of asshole is very protective of its nest, and will not hesitate to attack, if you've tread upon its pissing grounds. Given its tendency to be armed, great caution is advised.

Social Habits: This particular type of asshole is not a gregarious creature. With the exception of the Paranoid Wacko, the Controlling Jerk is perhaps the least sociable, of all the assholes to be found in nature. Having little to no social skill, they prefer the company of those similarly limited in their social abilities. Gun ranges and survivalist meetings, where grunts and monosyllables are acceptable forms of communication, are, perhaps, the only concessions to socializing, which this asshole might allow. In general, they do not want to be in the company of anyone they cannot control, so most normal social settings are confusing and unnatural to them. The give and take of regular social interaction is thoroughly alien to them, and so they will quietly do their jobs and earn their pay, day to day, so they can go back home and dominate their household. This tyrannical home environment is really the only social environment where the Controlling Jerk feels truly comfortable. Because they are in the habit of enslaving and imprisoning their mates, they are, sadly, known to be prolific breeders. Naturally, any child unfortunate enough to be born into his lair will quickly become a victim of this merciless asshole. Although tending to prefer female victims, they do not actually care about the age or gender of their prey, so long as they are weak-willed and cowed enough to submit to his control.

How to Repel Attack: If you have foolishly tread onto the Controlling Jerk's territory, then you will surely have put yourself in great peril. This type of asshole is the most territorial of all assholes. You could be attacked, at any moment, by a variety of weapons. It is recommended that you run, as fast as you can, until you have, at least, moved outside of the Controlling Jerk's firing range. Since they are usually spectacular shots, it is recommended that you continue to run, even beyond that point. Trying to intimidate or dominate the Controlling Jerk will probably not work, unless you have police backup and a long range assault weapon. The only way to repel this asshole's attack is by avoiding it. Being unadventurous by nature, you are unlikely to encounter or anger this type of asshole, in day to day life, unless you have intruded on their personal space, somehow, by moving in on their territory or on one of their slaves. If, however, you have been unfortunate enough to fall under the control of a Controlling Jerk and have now found yourself imprisoned in the wicked asshole's lair, then it is recommended that you remain calm. Do not provoke the asshole, by indicating your desire to escape. Remember, this type of asshole's greatest fear is losing his control, over others. So, don't say or do anything to antagonize this unpredictable creature. Wait for an opportune moment, and then make your escape. Be certain to get the authorities involved, after you have made good your escape, because the only thing the Controlling Jerk understands is authority. So, if confronted with law enforcement or serious legal consequences, they may give up and seek a new victim, rather than go to the trouble of contending with people less submissive than yourself. If they have Diabolical Sicko tendencies, however, they may not leave it at that. They may find new and sicker methods of regaining control over you. But, at least, if you can manage to escape to some faraway place and put the fear of God into them, you have a slight chance of escaping, for good, and ridding yourself, forever, from the sinister claws of this very dangerous asshole.

THE NARCISSISTIC DOUCHE

If you are asshole-watching beside the lake and happen to spy someone, admiring their own reflection in the still waters, then you have likely stumbled upon a  Narcissistic Douche. This strange creature lives in a world of complete self-absorption, unable to relate to other living creatures and incapable of seeing things from another point of view. All that matters to them is their own mirror image and their own wants and needs. Although not dangerous, they can be utterly exasperating in their complete lack of consideration for others. Neglectful of anything that does not have to do with themselves, they cannot be relied upon to be good friends, partners, lovers or fathers. It is advised that the cautious asshole-watcher merely observes the Douche, without approaching it or attempting to communicate, in any way. No association between a human being and a Narcissistic Douche has ever been a good one. It would only be an exercise in frustration and disappointment.

Likely Occupations: Professional Bodybuilder, Teen Pop Idol, Celebrity Playboy.

How to Identify: The Narcissistic Douche will always be immaculately coifed, with the newest clothes and irreproachable hygiene. Unlike your average well-dressed gentleman, the Narcissistic Douche does not take care of themselves as a sign of respect for others. They always look their best, because they love themselves enough to spoil themselves, and because they are so wholeheartedly obsessed with their own appearance. The natural habitat of this asshole could be a hair salon, or a classy social event, or even a high-end gym. Above all, you will never find the Douche engaged in any kind of dirty work, where they may get their hands dirty or their hair may fall out of place. Their vanity knows no bounds and so the best way to identify this variety of asshole is to observe how they react to their own reflection. If they stop to admire themselves, smiling lovingly, upon sight of their own face, then you will know that you have spotted a genuine Narcissistic Douche. By observing this reaction to reflective surfaces, you can make certain that you have sighted the genuine article, rather than simply a well-dressed man or a particularly good-looking human being. Actors, models and other individuals who need to look good, for their professions, are often mistaken for Narcissistic Douches, when they are actually normal human beings, just trying to make a living. For this reason, asshole-watchers can often have great difficulty in identifying the Douche. Be sure to look for the "mirror reaction" to determine if you have really found a Narcissistic Douche, rather than a regular human being.

Social Habits: The Narcissistic Douche is not very interested in others, but is usually quite sociable. This is because, although he may not care about you, as a person, he still needs an audience, to adore him. Much like the Arrogant Prick, this asshole needs to feel adored. But, unlike the Arrogant Prick, the Douche will usually not try to dominate you. He displays himself, in all his gorgeous greatness, and if you fail to acknowledge his exceptional qualities, then he will simply give you the cold shoulder. This type of asshole can easily develop a grudge and he will likely use every passive aggressive tactic in the book, to show you his disapproval, if you have been foolhardy enough to cast doubt on his perfection. He will spread lies, gossip and do everything in his power to convince his social circle that you are a horrible person and this is why you fail to appreciate his splendor. Because he loves to be admired, he is likely to be found in a highly social environment, such as your local country club, an exclusive restaurant or a popular nightclub, where he can strut around, in all his glory, and draw as many admiring stares as possible. Because they require their entourage for no other purpose but to reinforce their self-love, they will be very protective of their social circle. The inquisitive asshole-watcher may wish to examine the nearest social clique, where you are sure to find a Narcissistic Douche, in residence, doggedly guarding the group against anyone who may doubt the Douche's greatness or outshine him with even greater, more exceptional qualities. Narcissistic Douches may be mistaken for Pretentious Asses, because of their tendency to form exclusive social cliques. But, in reality, they have very little in common. Whereas the

Pretentious Ass will join an exclusive club to compensate for his own deep-seated feelings of inferiority, the Douche actually believes he is the greatest thing to ever walk the earth, and so believes he deserves an exclusive clique. See the section on Pretentious Asses for more details. This ability to distinguish between the Narcissistic Douche and the Pretentious Ass is the hardest part of learning to identify the Douche. If you are ever uncertain, then keep in mind the "mirror reaction," as defined earlier. The Pretentious Ass may stop to fix his hair, when passing a mirror, but he will lack the open-mouthed self-adoration and mirror-kissing that you'll see in the genuine Douche.

How to Repel Attack: A Douche attack is nothing to fear. In fact, they are perhaps the most innocuous and feeble of all the assholes, because they would never wish to engage in a conflict, for fear of dirtying their hands or messing their hair. They may, however, try to damage your reputation by use of oblique and underhanded social tactics. They could easily spread rumors or convince everyone in their circle that you are a terrible person. However, that is unlikely to influence anyone, outside of their insulated little clique. If you find yourself threatened by the Douche, merely threaten him, with anything at all, and he will quickly run away, tail between his legs. Of course, the story of your vile wickedness will surely be recounted, again and again, within his social circle, but it can be guaranteed that the douche will be too afraid to even speak to you, let alone attack you.

THE DIABOLICAL SICKO

In the darkest
and most
forbidding places
of the world,
lurks the dark
and sinister
creature, known

as the Diabolical Sicko. They brood in their murky,
sinister caves, setting their traps and lying in ambush
for their prey. The Diabolical Sicko is the most
dangerous threat to be found in the entire animal
kingdom. Bitter and vengeful, by nature, they often
spend years, plotting their cruel and insidious revenge.
These creatures have become so twisted and demented
as a result of so many years of nursing their petty
grudges, that they have been completely drained of
compassion, empathy or any of the other qualities,
which might prevent a regular human being from
executing a diabolical trap, in order to harm and
destroy their enemies. If the cautious asshole-watcher
ever suspects that a Diabolical Sicko is in the vicinity,
it is suggested that you proceed with great care. The

traps of this asshole have been known to be devilishly clever and horrifically cruel. Only the most experienced and skilled of asshole-watchers should attempt to approach them, because even being seen by the Diabolical Sicko could put you in harm's way, as anyone could become the subject of the asshole's next grudge, and the object of their next diabolical plot.

Likely Occupations: Intelligence Operative, Lawyer, Black Hat Hacker.

How to Identify: The Diabolical Sicko can be difficult to identify, because they are extremely resourceful assholes. Like the Shady Scumbag, they tend to hide in broad daylight, by camouflaging themselves and blending into the background. They will often appear to be entirely normal human beings. They are even more difficult to identify than the Shady Scumbag, because the Diabolical Sicko is the most intelligent of all the assholes. So, they are better at masking their true natures and obscuring their true intentions, than the Shady Scumbag. They are that disturbingly cold and systematic criminal, which you might have heard about, on the news--the one who has poisoned their enemies or ordered a hit on their ex, or spent years devising an intricate and fiendishly clever plot to frame somebody or ruin the reputation of someone who once wronged them. There is really no way to identify this dangerous asshole, because you will usually have no idea how big an asshole they are, until they have caught you in their trap. They could live in any environment and quickly adapt to new circumstances. The only way in which the perceptive asshole-watcher might be able identify the Diabolical Sicko is to observe closely and watch for signs of vindictiveness. The Diabolical Sicko is easily offended and will never forgive a slight. If they feel they have been disrespected, even if they have not been, they will never be able to let it go. If you observe someone react with a disproportionate amount of rage, in response to some relatively small slight, then there is a chance you have just identified the rare and elusive Diabolical Sicko. It is only at the moment the insult occurs, that the asshole will be too consumed by rage to conceal his true character, so this is the best opportunity to identify them. The Paranoid Wacko is also easily offended, but it is easy to differentiate between the two, because while the Paranoid Wacko will shout, rant and rave about how much you have offended them, the Diabolical Sicko will only be angry, at first. After they have cooled off a bit, they will then begin to execute their sinister plan for vengeance, at which point they will hide all evidence of their grudge or their intentions to seek revenge. At that point, there is no longer any way to identify them.

Social Habits: Diabolical Sickos can be either smooth and sociable, almost as much as the Slick Sociopath, or they can be extremely misanthropic loners. Depending on their personality, they are likely to be found in a variety of professions. The most sociable assholes may work as private investigators, intelligence operatives or any other career or organization that require high intelligence and a deep interest in covert and Machiavellian practices. The more solitary asshole is likely to be a black hat hacker, a designer of spyware and computer viruses, an unscrupulous entrepreneur or a fraudster. Above all, this asshole likes to be in a profession that stimulates their desire for passive aggressive power. They are not brave enough to meet their enemies, one-on-one, the way an Arrogant Prick might, and so they seek power in other, less overt ways. They are strongly attracted to fields such as law or politics, for this reason, and will often be found in powerful positions, from which they can easily wreak their vengeance on anyone who may be foolhardy enough to offend them. Of course, most of the people involved in these professions are regular, decent and hardworking human beings, but the keen asshole-watcher is advised to watch these professions, closely, as Diabolical Sickos tend to prefer these social habitats. It is important to remember that their primary motivation is revenge. If anyone shows them less respect than they think they deserve, then the Diabolical Sicko will live for no other reason but to exact their revenge. Given they are so easily offended, it is guaranteed they always have a score of active grudges going, at any given time, and so you can certain that vengeance is always the biggest thing on their mind. All social activity is geared towards increasing their de facto power, so they can be better equipped to mete out retribution, and so relieve some of the tension that has built up, over the years, as a result of the grudges that have been allowed to fester, in their sick and twisted minds.

<u>How to Repel Attack:</u> If you know yourself to be the victim of a Diabolical Sicko, then you can consider yourself lucky. Because most of their past victims probably didn't know what hit them. This type of asshole is smart enough to devise a truly insidious trap, to assure you are disposed of as thoroughly and surgically as possible. If you do find yourself in this situation, your only option is to run. Do not try to oppose them or fight back, because any contact with a Diabolical Sicko will result in tragedy. If a crime has been committed, then by all means, call the authorities, but never try to deal with this type of asshole, personally. As stated, this is the most dangerous of all assholes, so there is no recommendation that can be offered, to repel a Diabolical Sicko attack. The prudent asshole-watched is simply warned to watch out for vindictive and easily offended people, as stated above. Any account of a particularly cruel and malicious vengeance, having been perpetrated by the asshole, should be taken very seriously. A lot of the time, the only evidence of a Diabolical Sicko is a trail of previous victims, which reveal the pattern of vendetta, which is the Diabolical Sicko's entire life. By watching for some of these tell-tale signs, the asshole-watcher

might be able to avoid this asshole, altogether. Avoidance is really the only way to repel this asshole's attack.

THE SADISTIC BASTARD

The peaceful places of nature often appear serene and magical, to the average person. But, in reality,  they can often be brutal places, ruled by the cruel laws of nature. Lambs may frolic, under the protective eyes of their cute and fluffy mothers. But, in the same meadows lurk the cruel and merciless predators that will gladly eat a lamb for lunch. One of the most common of such predators is the Sadistic Bastard. This crude and primitive beast has no compassion for innocent lambs, fluffy, cute animals or anything else, for that matter. They derive pleasure from the suffering of others and are violent and stupid, by nature. If the adventurous asshole-watcher should wish to seek out the Sadistic Bastard, then they're advised to do so armed, because this variety of asshole is prone to sudden, unpredictable bouts of violence, and brute force is the only language their limited brain capacities are capable of understanding. Force will be needed to keep the Sadistic Bastard at bay, and so ensure a safe asshole-watching experience.

Likely Occupations: Sniper, Slaughterhouse Worker, Serial Killer.

How to Identify: The Sadistic Bastard usually has a distinctive sloping forehead, a dense, vapid look in his eyes and knuckles which are swollen from excessive knuckle-dragging and beating on things. A hint of drool is not uncommon. They are indisputably the stupidest of all the assholes in the animal kingdom. Occasionally, they are even stupider than supposedly lower life forms, such as rabbits and snails, but invariably have less complex personalities. They can often be spotted, exploding into fits of homicidal rage, because of some minor frustration, which a normal human being would be able to weather, with ease. This type of asshole can always be identified by their crude, expletive-laced bellowings and the violent shaking of branches and tearing of underbrush, which usually accompanies their demonstrations of temper. Having limited intelligence and no respect for others, they often have the distinctive scent of body odor and sport sweatpants, ball caps or any other article of clothing, which may be considered socially suicidal. They are attracted to the pain and suffering of others, so they may be found at correctional facilities, hockey matches, slaughterhouses or any other location where they can witness the physical punishment of sentient beings, firsthand. But, for the most part, the curious asshole-watcher need only listen for unintelligent-sounding voices and watch carefully for acts of sudden violence, in order to locate this all-too-common and dim-witted creature.

Social Habits: The Sadistic Bastard generally lacks social skill. Unlike regular human beings, who may be socially awkward because of shyness or a lack of experience, this variety of asshole is socially inept as a result of their stupidity, rather than any of these other causes. The thing you need to keep in mind, at all times, when dealing with this type of asshole is that they are really quite phenomenally stupid. And their violence is a method of compensating for their mental deficiencies. Whereas others might use charm, intelligence or a deep power of empathy, to get along with others and get what they need, from others, the Sadistic Bastard really has no resources, apart from violence. So, the violence of the Sadistic Bastard will always be based on their stupidity. The curious asshole-watcher may occasionally encounter a Sadistic Bastard who appears intelligent, but this will be nothing more than the most instinctual of mimicry. They may be able to learn basic sentence structure, in order to survive in today's fast-paced society, but their memorization of big words will be rote, and it is likely they will have no understanding, at all, about the meaning of the words they're using. If a Sadistic Bastard ever appears to be genuinely intelligent, however, then you may want to consider that you have made a misidentification. Arrogant Pricks and Diabolical Sickos can often be mistaken for Sadistic Bastards, due to their propensity for violence and cruelty. However, these varieties are far more intelligent than the Sadistic Bastard. Sometimes, a particularly stupid Arrogant Prick or Diabolical Sicko may also have a little bit of Sadistic Bastard in their makeup, making it even harder to make a positive identification. In order to avoid confusion, you need to examine the motives of the asshole you are viewing. If he seems to be quite stupid and seems to truly savor the suffering of others, then you are probably dealing with a Sadistic Bastard. Other varieties will be motivated by power or revenge or some other, less primal and primitive instinct. Always remember that the Bastard is a simple creature who must compensate for his deficiencies, by using violence, and the only time he ever feels adequate, is when he is watching a sentient being suffer, at his hands. Sadism, therefore, is their only motivation. The social habits of this asshole begin to show themselves early on, and the vigilant asshole-watcher can often observe them, near schools and playgrounds, playing the role of the schoolyard bully. Because of their limited mental skills, they rarely evolve beyond the schoolyard bully phase, and so are commonly found in prisons or the very simplest of manual labor jobs. The curious asshole-watcher is recommended to spend some time near the schoolyard, or the local prison, if they want to observe Sadistic Bastards in their natural social habitat.

How to Repel Attack: If you find yourself caught in the dull, torpid gaze of the Sadistic Bastard, then it is likely some dim thought of violence has entered their mind. Every time this asshole encounters a living thing, it is tempted to inflict violence upon it. If you find yourself in this situation, do not panic. Apart from their well-practiced fists, this variety of asshole is really not very formidable. They strongly favor weak and gentle targets, who are easily dominated. If you are well armed or are willing to fight back, in any way, they are likely to cease their pursuit and move on to more easily dominated prey. If, however, you have encountered a particularly tough Bastard, who is not dissuaded by your opposition, then you have only to outsmart the Bastard, in order to assure it never lays its paws on you. Contact law enforcement or security personnel, without delay, or use intelligence and social skill to open the Bastard up to social ridicule. The Bastard has no capacity to understand anything except violence, so they could well be intimidated by a cleverly-phrased bluff or by a well-thought-out social maneuver. Finally, if you do find yourself in the clutches of the Sadistic Bastard, close enough to smell its foul odor and feel the drool upon your face, then it is recommended you fight back, for all you're worth. Because, although they are naturally violent beasts, their lack of talent, in all things, extends to fighting, as well. The most sure fire way, therefore, to repel a Sadistic Bastard attack is to learn the art of self-defence. Knowing you are proficient, alone, will repel 90% of Sadistic Bastards, and your superior talents will help you effectively deal with the remaining 10%.

THE ATTENTION-SEEKING IDIOT

Listening to the sounds of the forest, at night, the knowledgeable asshole-watcher can learn to identify the various assholes, by  their call, alone. The deep, resonant call of the Arrogant Prick; the crude, guttural shout of the Sadistic Bastard; even, sometimes, the musical warbling of the Slick Sociopath. However, if you happen to hear a clear, strident cry, echoing with irritating frequency and marring the peaceful beauty of the night, then you have probably come within calling distance of the Attention-Seeking Idiot. Very common on the Internet, this brand of asshole lives for attention and hates nothing more than to be ignored. They will sometimes even degenerate into online trolls, seeking attention by any means necessary, whether positive or not. The inquisitive asshole-watcher can find them making a spectacle of themselves, in public places, or making an ass of themselves, on YouTube. They are generally not hard to spot, as they are already doing everything in their power to get your attention.

Likely Occupations: Shock Jock, Politician, Internet Celebrity.

How to Identify: The Attention-Seeking Idiot is easy to identify, as a result of his ceaseless noise and seemingly endless repertoire of attention-getting devices. What differentiates the Attention-Seeking Idiot from a regular attention-seeker is the fact they're willing to do anything, no matter how offensive or hurtful, to get your attention. The feelings and rights of the people around them mean nothing to them, in comparison to their need to be seen. No other asshole will be "in your face" quite as often, or as readily, as the Attention-Seeking Idiot. Unlike the noisy Arrogant Prick, however, or the imposing Sadistic Bastard, the Idiot will never actually behave in a threatening manner, except when they are online. Online, they are the notorious "keyboard warriors" who troll anyone and anything, in the hopes of getting your attention, through shock tactics. But, in the flesh, they are considerably less courageous. They may occasionally risk angering someone, if they consider the attention worth it, but they will never actually be willing to take chances, with their physical safety. That's how you can differentiate the Attention-Seeking Idiot from the other varieties of noisy assholes. They are known to frequent sporting events, public forums or anything that involves being exposed to large numbers of people. Although they are usually composed of decent, hard-working human beings, the fields of politics, radio and television broadcasting can sometimes be over-run by Attention-Seeking Idiots, who revel in the public platform and the ability to be heard by as many people as possible. Online, you can identify the Idiot mainly by his tactics. He is the one who intentionally shocks; the one who doesn't care how he gets followers, likes or attention, so long as he does get it--and as much of it as possible. He will have none of the refinement, discourse or even basic, human civility of the average Internet celebrity or video blogger. Such extreme attention-seekers and online trolls have been known to take their shock tactics to such extreme levels, online, that they have been subject to arrest and criminal charges. This is nature's way to eliminating the Attention-Seeking Idiot from the gene pool and ensuring he is not able to mate and reproduce his kind. Although it may seem cruel, to see a famous Internet star go to jail, or a "keyboard warrior" sent to the pen, where he must learn to contend with real-life warriors--it is important that you do not interfere. Nature may seem cruel, at times, but it's all part of the circle of life.

Social Habits: The Attention-Seeking Idiot is motivated only by attention, and nothing else. In spite of his name, he is not always an idiot. Some of them are quite intelligent. The clever Idiot might gravitate towards a field in politics, entertainment or any other highly public profession, which may require thought and talent. Of course, the vast majority of politicians and professional entertainers are wonderfully talented human beings, but the occasional intelligent Idiot could easily find its way into these professions, so the asshole-watcher is recommended to keep an eye on them. In spite of the occasional smart Attention-Seeking Idiot, the vast majority of them will be true idiots, in every sense of the word. And these less intelligent assholes will spend most of their time online, flaming people on social media or spamming comment boards with their vitriol. If they are of a more sociable turn, these stupider Idiots might venture away from their keyboard, and seek attention from the public. In which case, they will spend their days bar-hopping during football season or pouring beer over their heads, at the ball-park. Depending on the stupidity of the Idiot, he may have a tendency to get arrested for his shenanigans, either online or in public. This is why the curious asshole-watcher is advised to visit his local prison or penal institution, to observe the most idiotic of the Attention-Seeking Idiots, as that is where they invariably end up. In this situation, they are always the loudest and most obnoxious of the prison inmates. Of course, this kind of behavior could lead to a lot of trouble for the Idiot, in prison, but the less-gifted Idiot is not bright enough to see that, until it is too late. But, regardless of where you might find them--at city hall or in the city jail--this variety of asshole will be someplace where people congregate, as they are a very unimaginative and non-creative variety of asshole and see little point in living, without the stimulation and company of others. In a strange and twisted way, they are gregarious creatures, and will rarely be found living alone, in solitude. As a final point, the careful asshole-watcher is advised to take great care, if he ever finds two Idiots in one place. This type of asshole hates to be ignored and is accustomed to being the loudest person in the room. If he finds himself in the proximity of another Attention-Seeking Idiot, the resulting conflict could get quite violent. The meeting of Idiots, in this way, has been likened to a cock fight. They will circle around each other, eyes like daggers, and try to scare each other away, by use of cacophonous cries and dazzling displays of attention-seeking. The prudent observer is advised to stay well back and observe this awesome display, from a safe distance.

How to Repel Attack: The Attention-Seeking Idiot is not a particularly dangerous creature, by nature, but it will sometimes attempt to give the impression of power, by ruffling its feathers and arching its back. Especially online, the less intelligent Idiot will often try to simulate more powerful animals through creative use of profanity or by pretending that he's a formidable hacker, who is going to "mess you up" by hacking your Twitter account. However, in truth, this is nothing more than a clever bluff, which the Idiot has evolved, over centuries, to compensate for his debilitating stupidity. For this reason, the troll variety of this asshole is nothing to be feared, because they are inherently cowardly. Any real threat to their liberty or anonymity will cause them to instantly withdraw their abuse and head for the hills. If, however, you are the victim of a more intelligent Idiot, such as a vindictive politician or local celebrity, who has chosen to victimize you for the sake of attention, then you need only join them, in the publicity game and fire back, as skillfully and intelligently as you can. The Idiot doesn't like to fight directly with anyone who is able to fight back. Even the tiniest damage to their reputation, through your effective public retaliation will make them nervous and hesitant to attack you again. The worst thing that could happen to this particular asshole would be for the public to turn on them, and so make them pariahs. If shamed, in this way, they would lose all the celebrity they have carefully nurtured, and so lose their entire audience. That is a fate worse than death, to them. If the careless asshole-watcher does find themselves in the sights of the intelligent Idiot, one round of successful retaliation, in a public setting, will be enough to repel the asshole, forever.

THE PARANOID WACKO

Out in nature, the wild things run free and their constant activity makes the great outdoors a busy and active place. Carefree, the beasts and the cute little critters of nature frolic through the flowers. All, that is,

except the Paranoid Wacko. This type of asshole hides deep underground, tinfoil hat on their head, afraid to emerge into the bright light of day, for fear of the many dangers they imagine are out there, lying in wait for them. When they do venture out, they are constantly on the lookout for people who are trying to insult or disrespect them. The prudent asshole-watched is advised to watch his step, when approaching the Paranoid Wacko, for even the most innocuous word or well-meaning action might appear to be a threat, an insult or a sign of disrespect, in the twisted mind of the Wacko. He is that unbalanced psycho who thinks everyone is out to get him or that hair-trigger nut-job who thinks that you're talking about him. This oversensitivity to perceived insults and imagined slights is what make the Wacko such a tedious and unpleasant asshole. There are few other assholes, in all the animal kingdom, who are harder to get along with.

Likely Occupations: Factory worker, janitor, postal worker.

How to Identify: Apart from the occasional tin foil hat, the Paranoid Wacko is most easily identified by their furtive movements, their shifty eyes and their general look of defensive mistrust. If you have spotted such a creature, then you may have identified a Paranoid Wacko. To differentiate this asshole from the regular paranoid human being, you only need to examine how they react to the people around them. Whereas the average human, suffering from paranoia, might shy away from others and hide behind their living room curtains, the asshole will venture forth, shouting indignantly at every person who crosses their path, without saluting, and punching random stranger in the face, because they looked at them funny. Although they will not always take it so far, as to assault people, there is always the risk that their anger about imagined insults will reach the level where violence is likely. That is what makes them such terrible company and such a blight on the lives of anyone who is forced to coexist with them. The worst partners in the world, they will always assume their partner has been unfaithful to them, and refuse to believe their partner, if they deny it. On the contrary, they will become even more incensed, because now they believe they've been lied to, on top of cheated on. The same escalating cycle of imaginary wrongs will pollute any relationship the Wacko may have, making them not only the worst partners, but the worst fathers, sons, brothers, room-mates, business partners, or anything else, for that matter. There really is no way to win, with a Paranoid Wacko. No matter how kind, respectful and faithful you are, they will invent some wrong, which you have supposedly committed against them. When they have a bit of the Controlling Jerk or the Sadistic Bastard in their makeup, these assholes can be a real nightmare, for anyone who is unlucky enough to be in their life. If the daring asshole-watcher wishes to view the Paranoid Wacko, he is advised to check under rocks or in bomb shelters, as they generally prefer to stay hidden. However, they may occasionally emerge into daylight to attend a preppers' meeting or help spread the word about their favorite conspiracy theory.

Social Habits: The Paranoid Wacko does not socialize very often, even within their inner circle. This is because they do not trust anyone well enough to really let loose and be real. They are friendless, lonely creatures, but only because they refuse to trust anybody enough to make friends, and so they're not really to be pitied. Their fate is of their own making. And, unlike the paranoid human, they use their inherent distrust of other people to make people's lives miserable. They are likely to be found working on an assembly line, as a sanitation worker or any other profession that allows them to be alone, undisturbed and free to brood upon the many crimes that have been committed against them. This intense brooding and nursing of grudges is what the Paranoid Wacko does best, and so it is their constant preoccupation. At home, they may experience some very rudimentary bonding with family or friends, if these individuals share a belief in their favorite conspiracy theories.

Paranoid Wackos sometimes form superficial friendships with people who are paranoid about the same things they are. This is why they will occasionally be found in public, at meetings of conspiracy enthusiasts or survivalist conventions, where they can swap tips about how best to survive, when the apocalypse finally hits. Apart from these rare exceptions, however, the truly Paranoid Wacko will have very simple and predictable social habits. It will go something like this: you say something blunt, they take offense; you say something neutral, they take offence; you say something positive, they take offense; you say something wonderfully, mind-blowingly complimentary, they take offense. And, of course, if you say nothing, they will assume you don't like them or are ignoring them and, yes, you guessed it... they take offense. This invariable routine is what makes the Paranoid Wacko such a pain to be around and what qualifies them for a listing in our field guide to assholes. Unlike the regular, healthy human being, who makes an effort to put people at their ease, and so nurture social harmony, the Wacko cares nothing for others, but only cares about his fragile and easily-bruised ego. The asshole-watcher is advised to stay well outside of the Paranoid Wacko's hearing range, lest some innocent remark set off their natural paranoia and leave you open to one of their wild and raving attacks.

How to Repel Attack: If you are under attack by the Paranoid Wacko, then you have likely been foolish enough to open your mouth, in their proximity. Either that, or something about your very existence, here on Earth, has deeply offended the Wacko's sensibilities and hurt their pride. This kind of offensive existing is something the average asshole-watcher cannot do anything about, as erasing your existence, so as to placate the asshole, is not advisable. The Wacko is renowned for its fearsome growls and its horribly unpleasant roars, when once it has become enraged. However, try to stay calm. Keep in mind that the Wacko's greatest fear is to be disrespected. If you can bluff them into believing that you have great respect for them, this may be enough to stun the asshole, long enough for you to make good your escape. This maneuver must be done quickly, however, with consummate skill, as the Paranoid Wacko is completely untrusting and it will not believe you for long. Within moments, they will have decided that you are lying, and they will hate you with an even more ferocious intensity. Apart from this one trick, there is no easy way to repel a Wacko attack, and the prudent asshole-watcher is advised to simply avoid this type of asshole, and keep well out of its sight, in order to avoid an attack.

THE PRETENTIOUS ASS

If your asshole-watching takes you near the golf course, you may want to take that opportunity to observe the creature, known as the Pretentious Ass. Golf courses, country clubs and expensive  restaurants are usually teeming with Pretentious Asses and their distant cousin, the Narcissistic Douche. This type of asshole revels in looking down his nose at every lowly peon, which happens to cross his path. He is never happy unless he is somehow expressing his superiority over everyone around him. You can often see this asshole, in the city, driving luxurious cars, which he cannot afford, or disdainfully dismissing the service staff, at your local high-end martini bar. Whether he is rich, or merely making ends meet, the Pretentious Ass will always appear as if he is wealthy, well-bred and strictly at the very top of society's upper crust. Although ridiculously vain and ostentatious, the

Ass is, in fact, a deeply self-conscious creature, who feels he must appear superior, in order to cover up, and compensate for, his own feelings of self-loathing and his low self-esteem.

Likely Occupations: Socialite, Luxury Car Salesman, Stock Broker.

How to Identify: The Pretentious Ass is not too hard to spot. This creature has a tendency to keep his snout raised high and will generally be dressed in the most ridiculously elegant finery. They drive the best cars, wear the best brands and are generally designed to impress. They can be hard to distinguish from the Arrogant Prick and the Slimy Creep, sometimes, because they are all partial to luxury and rooster-like displays of ostentatious show. But the Pretentious Ass is unique, because it is the only asshole who is after social prestige, alone. They will not be as pushy as the Prick and have little interest in power and dominance. They generally lack the Prick's bravery and so they seek their power through passive means, like social status, and not brute force. It is unlikely they would ever get physical with you, for they have little confidence in their own abilities and are likely to be more scared of you, then you are of them. Also, unlike the Slimy Creep, who might buy a Ferrari in order to get dates, the Pretentious Ass buys it for entirely egotistical reasons. He may well use the car to help him get dates (only with socially acceptable women, of course) but that will be far from his primary motivation. The inquisitive asshole-watcher should bear in mind that the Pretentious Ass has only one motivation, and that is social advancement. So, if you have difficulty identifying the Ass, or distinguishing it from the Prick or the Creep, simply look to the places where the upper crust congregate. If you find a pretentious looking rooster, roaming the country club, nose in the air, then you can be fairly certain you have correctly identified the Pretentious Ass. And if you are still unsure, merely go up to the asshole and extend a hand. If he looks at your hand with a look of patrician, icy disdain, then you have, indeed, succeeded in your search for the Ass.

Social Habits: As stated, the Pretentious Ass is motivated by one thing: social advancement. So, given their purpose, nature has equipped them with a fairly impressive toolbox of social skills. The Ass will be capable of great persuasiveness, when he likes you or sees you as being useful to his social advancement. If you are a female asshole-watcher, with some claim to social distinction, you will need to be careful, as they are notorious for pursuing rich ladies, with a dogged determination and a well-practiced charm. Given that "marrying for money" is one of the most passionate interests of the Pretentious Ass, any female asshole-watcher, with means, is advised to stay well out of sight, when observing the Ass. They are often found in exclusive men's clubs or at the dinner parties of the rich and famous. These are the two most common social habitats of the Pretentious Ass. They will gravitate towards places where they can use their formidable social skills to help improve their social standing. In spite of this high level of sociability, which often enables the Ass to get married, have children, and have all the appearances of a normal human life, the asshole is actually incapable of forming real friendships. Because they are assholes, and not regular human beings, they will never have any actual interest in the people they meet. On meeting you, they will perform a quick mental analysis, determining your social status, and whether or not you can help their "career" as an obsessive social climber. Depending on the results of this internal analysis, they will either fawn over you shamelessly or turn their nose up at you and snort. But never, at any point, will they be interested in you, as a person. For this reason, the Ass is essentially friendless, no matter how many high-profile people surround them and so they will never know the pleasures of friendship or love, the way human beings do.

How to Repel Attack: If the Pretentious Ass has targeted you for social ridicule, it can only be because you have either worn the wrong shoes, in his presence, or because he has decided it will help him, socially, to make a victim of you. In either case, it is quite simple to repel the Pretentious Ass, and a variety of techniques are at your disposal. Being fundamentally cowardly, any threat of physical punishment will, of course, send them running. If you prefer not to resort to such methods, however, you need only keep in mind their psychology. The Pretentious Ass' primary fear is social embarrassment, and so you merely need to threaten them with some form of public humiliation, and they will quickly sever all ties with you. Asshole-watchers have occasionally found themselves victimized by the Ass, when giggling at his pretentions or otherwise making him feel socially inferior. The Ass will, occasionally, become so incensed by such a slight, that his natural inferiority complex will kick in, and he will not be able to hold back his rage. He will then do his feeble best to make an example of you. As stated, however, the Ass is not a formidable opponent and any threat, whether physical or social, will cause him to quickly withdraw.

THE SLIMY CREEP

In the spring, the birds and the bees come out to smell the flowers, and seek a suitable mate. Love is in the air, and all the world feels romantic and exciting. But, for one variety of  asshole, every day is spring, and they are always in the mood for love. The Slimy Creep is so renowned for its disturbingly obsessive libido and the excessiveness of its inappropriate romantic advances, that it easily ranks within the top five of nature's most irritating and obnoxious assholes. Common to strip clubs and singles bars, they are that sleazy jackass who just can't seem to open his mouth without saying something inappropriate or making a sexual reference. They are literally unable to have normal human relations with women and because they do not have the mental faculties to control themselves, in this way, they can be very dangerous to human females who might find themselves within their sight. The prepared asshole-watcher is advised to keep a mobile phone handy, when observing the Slimy Creep, because you may occasionally need to call the authorities. Their boorish behavior knows no limits and their harassment of women often crosses the line into the criminal. A call to the police or to animal control may be necessary, depending on what seems most appropriate.

Likely Occupations: Strip club owner, Construction Worker, Film Producer.

How to Identify: The Slimy Creep is easy to spot and the observant asshole-watcher can easily distinguish them by their reeking cologne, their tendency to wear gold chains and their prominently displayed chest hair. But even more apparent, will be their crude and aggressive behavior, towards women. Whereas the normal, healthy human male will tend to consider women to be human beings, of the female variety, and so perceive them to be appropriately complex and fascinating individuals, the Slimy Creep is too dominated by his freakishly excessive sex drive and his hopelessly deficient brain power to see women as anything but sex objects. Because of this, he will not be capable of behaving himself, in a normal human manner, when he is around them. Whether at a strip club, or on a dating website, he will invariably reference sex and be simply incapable of realizing that he is talking to a human being, who has many facets to them, outside of the procreative one. He will often drive expensive cars or possess various other status symbols, which are meant to augment his sex appeal. Unlike the Arrogant Prick, the Slimy Creep does not buy these status symbols for power and prestige alone. His only reason for anything he does is for sex. Because they think with their crotches, rather than their brain, they are not intelligent enough to understand the fact that few women are, actually, impressed by status symbols, alone. Any time that his efforts might fail to attract a mate, he will be completely perplexed and confused. However, this confusion will only last until the next time he sees a woman, at which point he will no longer be able to remember what happened yesterday. For this reason, it is rare to find this variety of asshole married. If they do marry, they will not be faithful for long. Divorce, on the grounds of infidelity, are a common identifying feature, for this asshole. If the intrepid asshole-watcher has trouble locating Slimy Creeps, in the wild, it is recommended that you try the local courthouse and observe the divorce proceedings. You are sure to find a Slimy Creep, before long.

Social Habits: Because of their obsession with sex, the Slimy Creep will be found somewhere sleazy, such as an adult accessories shop or your local red-light district. They like to socialize with men who share their particular brand of mental dysfunction, and that is why you will often find them in strip clubs or dirty movie theatres. They are very common in bars, however. And, much like their choice of partners, they are not very particular. They will go to any bar, so long as they can get drunk and make a total bastard out of themselves by hitting on every woman in the building. They can come across as fairly sociable, when in the company of men or close family members. But once you get them into the company of non-blood females of a marriageable age, they will reveal their true colors and quickly exhibit all the asshole qualities for which the Slimy Creep is famous. They will often be found working in strip clubs, as the loud-dressing, gold-chain-wearing manager or working as a film producer, in order to take full advantage of the hopeful starlets, who may be willing to do anything the asshole desires, just to get into movies. Although not usually intelligent or industrious, by nature, the Creep's deviant urges are so overwhelmingly powerful, that they will often act with extraordinary cunning, in order to fulfill their dreams. And so, you may find them working as bar managers, film producers, or any other area where you can be in a position of power, over women, in spite of the fact these positions usually require more intelligence than the Slimy Creep has at his disposal. Because of the intensity of their desires, they will usually grasp onto such a position like a bulldog, when once they have been fortunate enough to acquire it. This kind of position is, after all, the ideal social habitat for the Slimy Creep. The asshole-watcher is advised not to threaten the Slimy Creep's position, when they are in their ideal habitat, because they can be very protective of their territory. Libido-induced acts of barbarism are always a possibility, with the Slimy Creep, so it is important to approach them with caution.

How to Repel Attack: If you ever feel the clammy

paws of the Slimy Creep, anywhere on your body, then you are already in extreme peril. You have probably come close enough to the creature to smell its overpowering scent of cologne. This nostril-straining reek has been specially evolved, by the Creep, over centuries, to stun its prey and render them paralyzed, so that it can more easily reproduce its kind. If the terrified asshole-watcher has found themselves in this state of paralysis, with the hot breath of the Creep beast on their neck, then it is advised that you concentrate as hard as possible on raising your knee, at such an angle, so as to make contact with the aroused creature's groinal region. Since this is the location of the Slimy Creep's brain, this will render him senseless for a long enough time for you to get away. However, make sure the contact is violent enough to cause pain, otherwise the Slimy Creep may enjoy it. Failing this, however, there are still a few options for effectively repelling this asshole. The knowledgeable asshole-watcher will know that the Creep's biggest fear is being unattractive or sexually unappealing. So, if you find yourself encased in the stench of their cologne and see their slimy hands reaching towards you, you need only mention something to them, casually, which threatens their sex appeal. You could, for example, suggest they're developing a bald spot, or that a zit just popped up on their nose or that their toupee came loose. Either of these tactics will send them running to the nearest mirror, in a panic, and so allow you to make your escape, at leisure. You might also want to suggest that someone is breaking into their Ferrari, or that some woman, across the room, just had a wardrobe malfunction. Any of these ruses are guaranteed to dupe the feeble brain of the Slimy Creep, and so save you from their vile attack. It is strongly suggested, however, to any victim of the Slimy Creep that you report any serious sexual misconduct to the authorities, without delay. As stated, this creature is feeble-minded, as a rule, and only hard justice will be sufficient to penetrate their thick skulls, and so teach them sexual assault is wrong.

THE IGNORANT S.O.B.

Many horrible and venomous creatures haunt the dark places, ready to pounce on the hapless and unprepared asshole-watcher. Great care must be taken, to assure you don't fall victim to these fearsome beasts. The Sadistic Bastard or the Diabolical Sicko have been known to catch the asshole-watcher unawares, and so render them prematurely retired from the field of asshole-watching. A run-in with a Controlling Jerk or a particularly Paranoid Wacko could also lead you down the road to disaster. But no less unpredictable and dangerous is the Ignorant S.O.B. This creature resides in the very darkest corners of the world, subsisting entirely on a diet of hate. Hatred is the only thing they live for and, as a result, there is no opportunity for hatred, which they will pass up. If you are of a different religion, race or socio-economic bracket, they will hate you. Even if you think differently, dress differently or brush your teeth differently, that will be enough of an excuse for them to hate you. This variety of asshole is perhaps the most common variety, and can largely be blamed for the lamentable state of the world. The wise asshole-watcher will always keep their distance, as to even come within the sight of the Ignorant S.O.B. will be enough to elicit the wrath of its insatiable hatred.

Likely Occupations: Religious Extremist, Unemployed Blogger, Terrorist.

How to Identify: The Ignorant S.O.B. is usually a drab and uninspiring creature. They may wear a ball cap, a white undershirt and a ratty old pair of jeans. But they could just as easily be dressed in fine and expensive clothes. The S.O.B. can be found in any place and culture. And so, it is actually quite hard to identify them, by physical appearance alone. But no matter how derelict or unimpressive they may appear, they will always consider themselves to be the best class of person, in the whole wide world. And, by extension, they consider every other class of person to be their inferior. Because of this deeply held belief, you can always identify the Ignorant S.O.B. by their haughty, cocksure movements, their rigid and limited view of the world, and their tendency to see in black and white. A severe and disquieting look in their eyes is another dead giveaway. What you are seeing, in fact, is the swollen and festering hatred, which has usually become so massive and all-consuming, in the heart of the S.O.B. that they are unable to stop it from appearing, in their eyes. The observant asshole-watcher will learn to identify this congealed hatred in the eyes and so accurately identify the Ignorant S.O.B. even when they are trying to hide their wickedness, under a veneer of politeness. It is common to confuse the Ignorant S.O.B. with the Pretentious Ass, because they are both prone to look down on others, with disdain. But the Ignorant S.O.B. is a far more dangerous beast. Whereas the Pretentious Ass feigns superiority, in order to cover up his deep-seated sense of inferiority, the S.O.B. takes it to another level. The Ass may treat you like you're the dirt on his shoes, but his motivation is a desire to feel better about himself. The S.O.B. is motivated by pure, unadulterated hatred. He genuinely believes he is better than you and, unlike the Ass, when he implies he dislikes you... you can be sure he is telling the truth. In fact, you can be certain that he doesn't merely dislike you. Rather, his soul is a festering inferno of crashing hate-mountains, exploding into conflagrating hate-balls of hate, bigger and more wicked than you or any other normal human being could even live long enough to imagine. Because he is a thoroughly evil and wicked beast, the asshole-watcher is advised to never have close personal contact with the S.O.B.

Social Habits: The Ignorant S.O.B. will always stick to its own kind. Because he hates everybody who is not exactly like him, this limits his social options, considerably. He is capable of hiding his volcanic hate levels in order to interact with people, on the job, or in other areas where it can't be helped. But he will never have unnecessary contact with anyone outside of his group. If an Ignorant S.O.B. has been polite to you, or even friendly, you can be certain it is only an act, and they are actually hating your guts, deep down inside. Unless, of course, you are extremely similar to them, in every way. In this case, they will act genuinely friendly. But, even in this case, the S.O.B. still presents a danger to the asshole-watcher. Because they will soon test you, to determine if you are as prejudiced and bigoted as they are. They will drop hints, ask leading questions or otherwise just fish around for signs of a mutually shared bigotry. If they can't find any hatred in your soul, or if they discover you are hate-free, they will proceed to revile you with as much vitriol as if you were the member of another class, race or economic stratum. So, because they are only able to socialize with other bigots, this limits their social options even more. The Ignorant S.O.B. will always be in a purely homogenous social habitat, where everyone is just as bigoted as they are. If the foolhardy asshole-watcher wishes to infiltrate such an Ignorant S.O.B. social group, it is recommended that you wear a disguise. It will be necessary to dress, act and expound all the same beliefs as the S.O.B. colony, in order to walk amongst these creatures, safely, and without setting off their hair-trigger hate reactions. Great care is needed, however, to keep up the facade, until you have completed your observations. Because, much like Diane Fossey with the gorillas, any false move could lead to chest-beating and primal acts of violence.

<u>How to Repel Attack:</u> If an Ignorant S.O.B. has decided that you brush your teeth differently than "their people" do, or if they have uncovered your disguise and discovered you have infiltrated their community, then you may find yourself staring down the shotgun barrel of the S.O.B. creature's formidable hatred. This is a very dangerous and serious situation to be in, because the hatred of the S.O.B. can motivate them to acts of truly horrific violence. Of all the assholes, with the possible exception of the Diabolical Sicko, the Ignorant S.O.B. is the most dangerous and fearsome beast in nature. It is strongly advised to never get yourself near enough to the S.O.B. for him to launch an attack on you. If, however, you've been caught unawares or have foolishly tread near to the beast, then it is strongly advised that you run. The true wickedness of this creature's heart is one hundred times darker than you could ever imagine, so further engagement is not recommended. They could do far worse than simply assault you. If you are caught in a corner, and have no other choice, then, by all means, fight. But, unlike the Pretentious Ass or the Narcissistic Douche, this creature's hatred is fierce enough to make him a formidable opponent. He will

84

not yield to you, if he hates you, because it is a matter of principle, to him. The principles being, of course-- hate, hate and more hate. The unfortunate asshole-watcher who finds himself in this position is advised to run and then get the authorities involved, if possible, because nothing good ever came from a human being engaging an Ignorant S.O.B. directly.

QUICK IDENTIFICATION DIAGRAM

LOUD AND PUSHY ASSHOLES

A. **Sadistic Bastard**
   See page 45

B. **Slimy Creep**
   See page 72

C. **Attention-Seeking Idiot**
   See page 52

D. **Arrogant Prick**
   See page 10

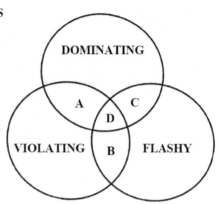

QUIET AND INTROVERTED ASSHOLES

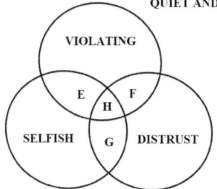

E. **Shady Scumbag**
   See page 15

F. **Paranoid Wacko**
   See page 59

G. **Controlling Jerk**
   See page 26

H. **Ignorant S.O.B.**
   See page 79

SOCIABLE AND CHARMING ASSHOLES

I. **Pretentious Ass**
   See page 66

J. **Slick Sociopath**
   See page 20

K. **Narcissistic Douche**
   See page 32

L. **Diabolical Sicko**
   See page 38

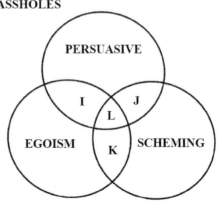

ASSHOLE-WATCHER'S CHECKLIST

Arrogant Prick

Date:_____

Where seen:_____

Notes:_____
_____
_____
_____

Shady Scumbag

Date:_____

Where seen:_____

Notes:_____
_____
_____
_____

Slick Sociopath

Date:_____

Where seen: _____

Notes:_____
_____
_____
_____

Controlling Jerk

Date:_____

Where seen:_____

Notes:_____
_____
_____
_____

Narcissistic Douche

Date:_____

Where seen:_____

Notes:_____
_____
_____
_____

Diabolical Sicko

Date:_____

Where seen:_____

Notes:_____
_____
_____
_____

Sadistic Bastard

Date:_____

Where seen:_____

Notes:_____

_____

_____

_____

Attention-Seeking Idiot

Date:_____

Where seen:_____

Notes:_____

_____

_____

_____

Paranoid Wacko

Date:_____

Where seen:_____

Notes:_____

_____

_____

_____

Pretentious Ass

Date:_____

Where seen:_____

Notes:_____
_____
_____
_____

Slimy Creep

Date:_____

Where seen:_____

Notes:_____
_____
_____
_____

Ignorant S.O.B.

Date:_____

Where seen:_____

Notes:_____
_____
_____
_____

ABOUT THE AUTHOR

Alexei Maxim Russell is a writer of fiction and non-fiction. His work tends towards Fantasy, Crime fiction, Folklore and Philosophy. His debut novel, Trueman Bradley, was published in 2011 by Jessica Kingsley Publishers. His other books include Why Not-World, Instruction Manual for the 21st Century Samurai, the New Home-Owner's Guide to House Spirits and the Forgotten Lore series. Read more about Alexei's books at www.whynot-world.com.

CPSIA information can be obtained
at www.ICGtesting.com
Printed in the USA
LVOW04s1504210416

484696LV00042B/629/P